"I construct a poem as if I was choreographing a ballet piece. Words twirl, jump, fly and I dance with them in uncensored abandon."

DONA ELENA HATCHER

Word Dances

POEMS
On Pointe!

DONA ELENA HATCHER

Introduction

I must acknowledge all the Wordsmiths who dare to share their thoughts, their imaginations, and their secrets. Those who dare to bare their feelings, their heart and soul.

Putting this book together, a lifelong goal, was extremely hard for fear of exposing all things mentioned above. I feel trepidation even now as to how my writings will be perceived, will they be understood and are they good?

There are a few things I want you to know about this collection. Every poem I write is an experience I actually had, someone I really know, something I saw or heard, or a feeling I felt. Of course, I sometimes use a variety of creative licenses and liberties but conservatively.

Being an Artist, I didn't want these pieces to look the same by being in the same font and style. That's more for novels and looked boring to me, so I mixed it up a bit. It's my style of presenting my creative writings. Please accept my apology in advance for poems I chose to print in all caps. I promise I am **NOT YELLING**! I simply like the way it looks sometimes!

Those with literary knowledge will quickly see that many of my poems are not written classically. Some rhyme, some don't. Some have mixed rhythms like a jazz piece or a modern, creative or contemporary dance that makes you feel something yet leaves question marks. These are my choreographed written word interpretations of various aspects and nuanced thoughts in my everyday life.

I'd like to thank my family, teachers, friends, and all the poets and people I have learned from. I'm so grateful to all who believed in my talent with words to convey feelings and inspire thought. I'm thankful to you who chose to read my book.

Enjoy!

Peace Please!

Dona Elena Hatcher

Contents

Ocean Watch

Nature's Best

Uptown Sites

THOUGHTS & DREAMS

LOVERS LOVE

OTHERS

LOSS & PAIN

WOMEN OF COURAGE

Ocean Watch

Waves

SEEING EACH ONE GO BACK AND FORTH
I WISH THEY WOULD TAKE ME WITH THEM
BUT THEY DON'T. THEY WON'T.
THEY LEAVE ME STANDING ON THE SHORE
WITH THE SUNRISE AND THE SUNSET
I SIT THERE WITH THE REJECTED SHELLS
THE DEJECTED SHELLS
WANTING. WONDERING.
WHY DON'T THEY TAKE ME?
WHY DON'T THEY WANT ME?
THEY'RE LAUGHING AND SPLASHING NOW
THEN THEY'RE THRASHING AND LASHING HOW?
SO STRANGE.
WAVES WILL COME TOMORROW AND AGAIN
BUT I WON'T.

Atlantic City at Night – The Waves

They seem to come from nowhere
Those waves rumbling in from the dark
The white crests arrive in a fury
They coil and slap each other then disappear on the edges of the sand
The black-blue of the horizon blends seamlessly together with the
    Ocean somewhere deep out there
With no beginning or end, silver ripples constantly appear before my
    eyes like sparks going off in the dark
And the ever-present sound, the thunderous sound that waves make
    only at night roars on and on and on
Blocking out the noise of the casino money machines
Striking out the suggestions, the smoke, the sleaze
Wiping out the rest of the world it seems
There is no better place for me to be
There is no other reality
Than right here on the beach by the deep dark sea
Letting loud, mysterious waves perform for me.

2

Atlantic City at Night – The Chair

And here I sit, playing Life Guard in the Chair up in the air
Having watch over the lonely stretch of darkness, ruling people of the
    night - this feels right!
Belonging to this scene so serene between the seductive sea and
    greedy casinos behind me

Every now and then, shadow people appear out on the sand
Walking or playing they think they understand the nature of life, of
    love, as I judge them from above
Tonight, I pretend to guard them, to guide them as I hide from ALL up
    there in the shadows of the Lifeguard Chair

It's so magical and peaceful late at night by the sea in AC
That I declare all subjects must be happy, must be free
Feeling love, giving love and knowing peace
Especially those here with me on the beach

Yes, I'm **Queen of This Night** holding court up in the air
Regally sitting in the shadows of the Lifeguard Chair

Deep Sea Love

COME ON AND TAKE A DIVE WITH ME
LET'S PLUNGE INTO THE DEPTHS OF THE SEA
WE CAN EXPLORE DEEP UNKNOWNS TOGETHER
AND MAY JUST FIND A HIDDEN TREASURE

HERE, LET'S PRY OPEN THIS CHEST
LET'S GATHER THE GEMS INTO OUR NEST
I WANT TO LINGER, LOOK, WANDER AND WONDER
MAYBE WE'LL DISCOVER HEAVEN UNDER WATER

NEW THINGS TO SEE AND TOUCH AND KNOW
TOGETHER WE CAN FIGHT OFF EVERY FOE
WHAT BEAUTY IT WOULD BE FOR YOU AND I TO KNOW
AND SHARE UNKNOWN SECRETS OF WHAT'S BELOW

COME ON LOVE, WE MUST MOVE FOR THE SEAS ARE WIDE
LET'S ALWAYS SWIM ON AND SIDE BY SIDE
SUBMERGING AND FLOATING ALONG WITH THE TIDE
IF YOU EVER CHOOSE TO LEAVE, I'LL MAKE ONE PLEA
DON'T LEAVE ME ALONE AT THE BOTTOM OF THE SEA

Nature's Best

Morning

Cheery Chirping Birds
Mornings Only Sound
Until My Thoughts Start Banging Around

Summertime

Summertime – Can't wait
What a joy for me to wake
To blue skies everyday
And strong sun where I can bake
My caramel skin to burnt umber
Glowing after months snowed under

Summertime – Must wait
Nine long months for three
To shed layers of needed clothes
And have my body feel free
Folks seem to smile for no reason
That's why I love each summer season

Summertime – Worth the wait
To swim and sail and stay out late
On sultry nights, the days are longer
Bar BQ, Watermelon and ice cream
All this, all winter I wait and I dream
For summertime and ALL it means

My Backyard Grass

Only two weeks left in October and we know what that means
Just a short time left to wear the uniform color of bright green
All summer long looking like a vacuumed carpet, neat and clean

Now struggling to hold onto one solid color shade
Along the edges the vibrant tone has begun to fade
Plus the torn out tufts the busy rodents have made

Poor grass, its best friend the sun, slowly moves farther away every day
The other friend the tree, now drops leaves of every color all over
    so carelessly
And those squirrels dig more holes since they can't find treats they
    hid yesterday

My once proud, pristine backyard grass is quickly losing its desired
    identity
Knowing all too soon it will surrender to wearing the drab green and
    dead brown cloak until spring
When the friends and the gardeners come back to tend it again

Beauty in a Hard Place

I see you! Sticking out in all your natural beauty.
Standing tall in the midst of chaos and disorder. Delicate and strong.
Doing nothing but what you were meant to do. Being where you are.
I'm always grateful to experience surprises. God's gifts.
I almost missed you. I bet most people do in this unlikely location.
Many might see but not see you. No one to care for or
about you. Most would step on you if need be.
But here you are. Thriving well between a rock and a hard place.
Having nothing you should have in order to grow. But you do.
You are a Success right where you are.
Pretty wild flowers growing in cement along
a brick wall in a dirty parking lot.
As I see you, I'm so inspired and encouraged about life.
We really were created to bloom and give
joy regardless of our circumstances.

Whooshh!

Wednesday, Wind Witch of the West – whizzed and whirled wildly wherever she wished without warning. WHOOSHH!

What a wicked warrior! Willingly wielding weapons, waging war, while weak wardens watched warily.

Whacking, wrecking at whim whatever wavered, with wild, wanton ways. WHOOSHH! WHOOSHH! WHOOSHH!

What's wrong with this warped wretched woman whipping up winding whirlpools?

Wounded, whaling witnesses winced. Wondering, waiting while windows whistled with waves of worsening wind.

WHOOSHH! WHOOSHH! WHOOSHH!

We would want and welcome a waltz with warm, whispering, whimsical winds while we waited we wondered

Why wrathful, wicked, Wind Witch of the West waged war with us and **WON** Wednesday?

A Moment with a Mole

Thoughtlessly turning into my backyard
I heard noises that sounded odd
A sort of scratching small animal sound.
Before I could blink or begin to think
The critter flew by me in a single bound
Disappearing swiftly in the bushes
But there was one strange split second when our eyes locked
Sensing to each other, no harm, no foul.
I experienced a very special moment with a mole

A Sudden Storm

I barely notice the few surprising sparkly flakes floating across my eye
Since no snow is expected, what's up in the sky will surely fly on by?
Tiny tufts of fluff fluttering about everywhere instantly melting on
contact
I'm following the path to my new home; I'm right on track - that's a fact

Pretty soon it was quite clear; the flurries planned to stay here
Fast in a flash, a swirling, dusty layer of snow instantly appeared
With the wrong shoes on I make crunchy impressions with each step
Trotting along a little faster now needing to beat the unwanted home

Already I can't see. There shouldn't be a blizzard so how could this be?
Quite quickly those puffs turned to clumps hitting and beating up on me
Glistening flakes feel like shards of glass, stabbing my ears, making my
eyes tear
I step up my pace holding onto confidence as life slaps me in the face

Suddenly, my feet start to glide; I slip, trip and begin the slide down
To hit the hard ground, dropping my pride and getting turned around
Faster and farther I go beginning to roll and all I want is to settle in
my home
Before, so sure. What is going on? How'd I wind up in an unanticipated
storm?

Over and over hard sticks and stones I blaze by spots I've never known
Unable to stand for long as strong gusts push to keep me from moving on
Enduring in a state of amazement, my life is frozen in shock and fright
I can't exercise my own free will but with grace I keep my goal in site

So unprepared was I for this sudden serious turn of events
It's futile to resist so I try to breathe, stay calm and persist
It's hard not to worry how I'll ever find my way back to my home
That I don't know, but in faith, straight ahead I'm determined to go

One Blade of Grass

One blade of grass glistening in the morning sun
All alone it knows no one
Far across the lawn where other grasses grow
Lies a life that it will never know

UPTOWN
SITES

.

Stray Dogs

Stray Dogs, Dirty Dogs, roaming like rats round the hood
Tongues hanging out, drooling in anticipation of something good
Barking absurdities and obscenities at *every* passing womanhood

Dirty, nasty Dogs, scratching their privates in full view
Peeing up against walls like that's just what men do
Daring to wag a mangy tail wanting someone to play with you?

Stray, stinky Dogs, scarfing down food on the street
Dirty paws in greasy tins trying to eat with rotted teeth
Begging strangers for a nickel a dime to buy crack or cheap wine
Don't even seem to mind because, somehow they still think they're fine!

All day and all night watching the block for what for who?
Running from 'responsibilities' and 'the man' as if on cue
Lying down wherever with whomever to rest your empty head
Just too lazy to do what you need to do to keep a steady bed

Hanging in packs ready to pounce with something slimy to say
And don't get why women wince and want doggie to just **Go Away!**
So lost and confused life must be hard out there for a Stray

No place to call home, no hope, you seem destined to roam
With your tail between your legs you'll fight to death over a dry bone
Wild red rimmed eyes always scanning, scamming to break the law
Poor, pathetic, matted men acting just like dirty, Stray Dogs

The Heights – Thought 1

When I first moved to the 'Heights' uptown
'Reggaeton' extra loud was the prevailing sound
Every block was steaming, my neck was snapping around
Ogling all those boys whose skin was bronzy brown

Shiny black hair, the barbers' lines fresh – precise!
The shirt's a tad *too* tight but those jeans fit just right
Cologne on strong and flashing those pearly whites
You just know I flirted and sashayed around town
Getting whistles from boys with skin bronzy brown

And when they spoke to me in their sexy Latino tongue
I was done! Couldn't care less that they were **ALL** too young
The hidden Cougar emerged as I purred to my hot new Amigo
"Hey Papi, tu quieres vai a mi casa conmigo"?

Ummm, I'm so glad I moved up to this part of town
To the Heights where the boys' skin is bronzy brown

The Heights – Thought 2

"They, Them, Those People"
I Sound Like a Racist!

Look at all **those** happy, grinning foreign faces
Filling up shopping carts as fast as **they** can
Just living the hi-life here on my fore-family's land

Yapping on phone cards back home to shores **they** adore
All ages pushing out babies not two but three and four
Knowing that US welfare will make sure **they** are all cared for

See how **they're** dressing – all matched up and blinged down
With subsidized rent, food stamps plus jobs underground
No wonder **they** can buy extras and party all around town

Many of **them** love to work, will do anything and keep a job or 2
Some are driving hoopties, vans, new SUV's but can't fill out a W2
How'd **they** get a license to sell these goods on a NYC street?
Making enough cash from Americans to send back home and keep

They eat **their** native food and speak **their** native tongue
They tend to hire and marry **their** own kind and date us just for fun

Just look at **them** laughing, loving, and living the American dream
They all have more than me now so it makes me want to SCREAM!
Oh America, America, the bountifull land of liberty
It really hurts to know you love **them** more than **ME!**

Shadow Man

Could be anyone
Everybody knows, nobody knows
He can take you by surprise
Everywhere you turn – there he is
You never know where to go NOT to see him
Not to fall under his spell if you do
You can't be too careful
He's over there and then here
Hauntingly
Hunting
Just for you
He's the innocent, the sweet
The strong, the weak
The tall, the short
Dark or light
Wrong or right
Day or night
You don't know how to avoid the **SHADOW MAN**
He's all around in shadows and he'll GET YOU
If he can.

Fallen Feather

Fallen Feather – Lost, Lonely, Dislocated, Discarded,
Left Behind. Disengaged From Its Root Source
First Drifting Freely About Here, There, With No Care
At Some Point, It Settles Softly Somewhere
Once Useful, Once Handsome – Now Dirty, Discolored
A Single, Shriveled Feather Seen in Wrong Places
Always a Little Sad to Me

Sometimes, I Pick One Up, Imagining Its Plush Past
I Dust It Off, Gently Wash, Dry and Try To Fluff It Up
Anticipating Future Possibilities, To Adorn A Special Place
But Soon I See, My Found Feather Has Failed Me
Too Light to Stay Grounded Long, It Becomes Burdened Down
With Atmospheric Dust and Outdated, Abstract Opinions
It Can't Hold Up, Can't Fulfill My Hopes, It's Far Too Weak
Too Damaged From Being Rejected, Ignored, Unaccepted

So I Give It Back To The Streets From Whence It Came
I Set It Free To Float or Get Stuck Again In Wrong Places
So Disconnected From Its Original Root Source
A Single, Shriveled Feather – Always A Little Sad To Me
Farewell My Fallen Feather Friend, Fare Well

Beer for Breakfast

EVERY SATURDAY MORNING, A FINE BUT BLEARY EYED BROTHER WAKES IN HIS DARK RENTED ROOM THAT WREAKS OF STALE CIGARETTES, ROACH SPRAY AND SOUR SWEATY SHOES

GRABBING LAST NIGHT'S CLOTHES FROM THE FLOOR, HE PUTS THEM ON HIS FRAIL BODY, THEN SELECTS A HAT AND SHADES OF COURSE

BAD BREATH AND ALL, HE HUSTLES DOWN THE HALL AND OUT THE DOOR WITH A QUICK STEP AND A FEW STUMBLES TO THE CORNER STORE

THROWING A FEW CRUMPLED BILLS ON THE COUNTER FOR HIS BREAKFAST, THE DELI MAN KNOWS THE SCORE

A COLD QUART OF THE CHEAPEST BEER, NOTHING MORE. A BREW FOR BRAKFAST IN A BROWN BAG WITH A STRAW

HAPPY NOW, GRINNING EAR TO EAR, HE SAYS TO ME, "GOOD MORNING SISTER DEAR"

I RESPOND, 'HOW ARE YOU?' - AND HE TOOK THAT AS HIS CUE…WELL, "IT'S MY DAY OFF AND I HAVE LOTS OF ERRANDS TO DO STARTING OUT WITH A LITTLE ALCOHOL WILL HELP ME GET THROUGH

BESIDES ITS ONLY BEER — THAT DON'T HAVE NO EFFECT ON ME. IT'S NOT LIKE DOWNING GIN AND JUICE OR LONG ISLAND ICE TEAS…

I DRINK BEER FOR BREAKFAST, LUNCH, DINNER AND ALL NIGHT TOO BEEN DOIN IT MY WHOLE LIFE AND PLAN TO CONTINUE, I'M 62!

I DON'T GOT NO PROBLEMS, I KEEPS A JOB, AIN'T THAT GOOD ENOUGH FOR YOU?

COME ON, LET ME BUY YOU BREAKFAST? A NICE, ICE COLD BREW!

HOW BOUT A BEER IN A BROWN BAG WITH A STRAW FOR YOU TOO?"

'UHHH', I MANAGE TO MUMBLE BACK… 'THANKS, BUT, NO THANK YOU.'

Thoughts & Dreams

A Poem for Right Now

The Corona Virus 2020/ Covid 19

Right now, I want **to be with** people I know
People that make me glow, that make me squeal Oh No! Is that so?

Right now, I want **to see** that smile **with my eyes**
Yours say what you can't disguise while we **in person** co-empathize

Right now I'd love **to touch** a familiar arm, a face
To share a **hug** an **embrace**, **feel** our hearts beat at the same pace

Right now we must stay **home in** our own space
Right now I implore, what's happening to **the Human Race?**

Silent Night Dream

SILENT NIGHT, LONELY NIGHT
SNOW IS FALLING
ALL AROUND
SNOWING ME IN
INSIDE MY HOUSE
INSIDE MY HEAD

I STARE OUT AT THE SOFTNESS
IT LOOKS LIKE A BABIES BLANKET
USED FOR WARMTH AND SECURITY
BUT I SEE THINGS THAT AREN'T TO BE
FOR ME THIS STORMY NIGHT

I IMAGINE I HAVE A LOVER WATCHING WITH ME
TOGETHER WE STEAM UP MY WINDOW PANES
WHISPERING SECRETS TO EACH OTHERS EYES WE SMILE
WISHING EVERY NIGHT COULD FEEL LIKE THIS ONE
WARM, SAFE, STILL, FILLED WITH PASSION AND LOVE

PLACING MY FINGER TO HIS FULL LIPS I QUIETLY SAY,
"LET'S LISTEN TO SILENCE, LET'S JUST BE AND SHARE MINDS
LET'S PRETEND WE HAD YESTERDAY, A DREAM AND NOW
TOMORROW, WE'LL MAKE FOOTPRINTS IN NEW SNOW".

SILENT NIGHT, LONELY NIGHT
SNOW KEEPS FALLING HEAVILY
ALL AROUND
AROUND MY HEAD
AROUND MY HEART
SNOWING ME INSIDE MY HOUSE ALL ALONE
AND ONLY WITH MY DREAMS TONIGHT
AND TOMORROW; THERE WILL HAVE TO BE
ONLY ONE SET OF FOOTPRINTS IN THE SNOW

"A Message to You"

I've been meaning to tell you that I don't get much rest
How could I? You won't let me catch my breath
Radio, computer and TV running 24/7
My lights kept on even when you're not home
I have no privacy, very little time alone
You are always doing something in my space
When 5 other rooms could easily take the place
All are functional and decorated in pleasing hues
But it's not just you, it's your crazy cats too
Who run and play leaving toys and hair on my floor
You bring everyone to me who comes through the door
I'm tired, I feel over used and a little bit abused
Even late night you'll stay, your bedroom you refuse
I'll give you credit, you do keep me shiny and clean
Always dusting and running that loud electric machine
You make me smell good with incense, candles and sprays
When I think about it, I probably shouldn't complain
People say I'm beautiful, filled with lovely things and good vibes
I host nice people, you like me most, I hold in secrets you confide
I'm your living room, your life, I keep you safe from evils outside.

If Only for a Day

IF ONLY FOR A DAY
WOULD YOU KNOW WHAT TO SAY? WOULD I?
WE WOULD HUG AND KISS
WOULD WE LAUGH OR CRY?
WHERE WE WERE CUT OFF IS WERE WE WOULD BEGIN
BUT HOW COULD WE LET THAT DAY COME TO AN END AGAIN?
IF WE HAD ONE MORE DAY DAD,
HOW MUCH WE'D HAVE TO SAY
IF ONLY...WE HAD ONE MORE DAY.

Daddy and Me

Before My Very Eyes

Before my very eyes
Dark clouds minimize
Pink, mauve and yellow skies ENERGIZE
Before my very eyes

Each blink makes a difference
Between what I saw and what I now see
Between what was us and what's now only me

The moon and the seasons CHANGE
As did what I thought and what I think
And how I felt and how I now feel about YOU

Old thoughts turn Gold
Sad thoughts turn Glad
Blue thoughts turn new about YOU

With a blink of an eye
Things change like the skies
About you, I am REVITALIZED
Before my very eyes

A Fantasy

WHAT A FANTASY
A FANTASTIC STORY MADE JUST FOR ME
BUT NOW IT'S FINISHED. I'VE REACHED THE END.
IT'S TIME TO CLOSE THE BOOK
I CAN'T EVEN GIVE IT A SECOND LOOK
NO MORE DREAMING OR SCHEMING
NO MORE TRYING TO CONVINCE ME, CONVINCE YOU
OUR LOVE FELT TRUE BUT NOW WE ARE THROUGH
IT WAS A STORY IN A BOOK OF FAIRY TALES
JUST A FANTASY
A FANTASTIC STORY LIVED BY YOU AND ME

LOVERS
LOVE

River Running or Mitch from LA

YOU'RE LIKE A POWERFUL RIVER RUNNING THROUGH THE LAND OF LIFE CONTINUOUSLY. NEVER STOPPING TO REST, TO ENJOY, TO THINK, TO LOVE.

HESITATING ONLY FOR A BRIEF MOMENT TO EASE OVER A ROCK, A STONE, A PIECE OF WOOD OR WHATEVER.

FLOWING QUICKLY OVER IT, UNDER IT, AROUND IT, THROUGH IT ANY WAY YOU CAN TO KEEP MOVING AHEAD.

SURGING ON TO OTHER PLACES, FAR AND WIDE, FAST OR SLOW, ANY FLOW WILL DO A MAN WITH NO PLAN, NO CARE, NO GOAL BUT TO PUSH FORWARD.

OVERTAKING EVERY THING IN YOUR PATH, ROLLING ON, GENERATING POWER, HEAT, DESIRE, NEED, SPEED.

FEEDING LIFE WITHOUT KNOWING IT, TAKING LIFE WITH NO GUILT ABOUT IT.

DRAGGING ANYTHING LESS STRONG ALONG FOR THE RIDE TO MEET ITSELF SOMEWHERE. ANYWHERE. YOU DON'T CARE!

YOU MAKE YOURSELF SMALLER OR LARGER AND LOSE YOURSELF IN YOUR OWN MINDLESS MISSION OF PERPETUAL MOTION.

YOU PASSED THROUGH ME WITHOUT PAUSE INTO OTHER MOVING WATERS OF ETERNITY.

Stone Man

I'M A STONE MAN!
"OH HE'S SO PROUD HE SAYS IT LOUD". **I'M A STONE MAN!**
SOLID AS A ROCK, INSIDE AND OUT, BOTTOM TO TOP.
I'M TOUGH AS NAILS AND SMOOTH AS STONE.
YOU CAN'T BREAK ME. I'M GOLD IN THE BONE.
EVERYTHING BOUNCES OFF ME. I AIN'T NO MAGNET.
I'M COOL. I NEVER SWEAT. I DON'T EVEN GET WET.
SHIT JUST WON'T STICK. CAUSE I'M JUST THAT SLICK!
I DON'T BEND, TWIST OR TURN.
I AM PERFECT JUST AS I AM. **A STONE MAN!**

AS YOU SEE, I CAN'T BE SCRATCHED BY YOUR WRATH OR
   STAINED BY YOUR TEARS.
AS **A STONE MAN**, I CAN'T CALM YOUR FEARS AND I WON'T
   SOFTEN UP WITH YEARS.
I'M LIKE STONE MOUNTAIN, THE STATUE OF DAVID. YOU
   CAN'T MOVE ME.
INPENETRABLE IS THE SCORE! YOU'LL NEVER REACH MY CORE.
YOU WON'T EVER KNOW ME AND I CAN'T BE OWNED.
YOU CAN'T MAR ME NO MATTER WHAT. THINK OF THICK
   MARBLE MA.
I'M COLD TOO BOO, SO I WON'T FEEL THE WARMTH OF YOUR
   LOVE.
CAN'T GIVE IT CAUSE I DON'T KNOW IT. COME ON MISS,
   WHAT'S THE DIF?

NOW YOU KNOW **I'M LIKE STONE** BUT I'M JUST WHAT YOU NEED.

BE ASSURED, I DON'T' PLAY, NOR WILL I STRAY. THAT'S WHAT I SAY!

I'LL CALL YOU BABY, LOVE, MY DEAR. THAT'S WHAT YOU WANT TO HEAR

I KNOW I WEIGH HEAVY ON YOUR MIND ALL THE TIME.

LOOK, I'M SOLID AND PROUD SO I SHOUT IT OUT LOUD.

I'M A STONE MAN! TAKE ME IN IF YOU CAN…HA HA

YOU KNOW I'LL ROCK YOUR WORLD BABY GIRL BECAUSE I AM

THE BEST, THE BIGGEST, HARDEST, LONGEST LASTING LOVER YOU EVER HAD.

YOU KNOW YOU'RE GLAD YOU GOT A CHANCE TO GET WITH ME. YOU SEE,

I'LL MAKE YOU SCREAM! I'LL TREAT YOU AS MY WOMAN, MY QUEEN.

AFTER YOU ACCEPT ME AS YOUR GOD!

"MY WHAT?"

Guy – The Beginning

WHY AM I THINKING SO MUCH ABOUT YOU
WHEN I TRY TO ACCEPT THAT THIS IS TABOO
YOU ARE FORBIDDEN FRUIT SO SHINY AND RIPE
I WANT TO BE WITH YOU ALL DAY AND ALL NIGHT
I PUSH YOU AWAY WHEN I WANT YOU TO STAY
OH COME ON, I'M JUST TRYING TO PLAY
YOU ARE NOT THE ONLY MAN IN MY LIFE
BUT YOU ARE THE ONLY ONE WITH A WIFE
AND I WANT YOU MOST ALL, OF COURSE
SO WHENEVER YOU'RE READY, TAKE ME, I'M YOURS

Guy – The Middle

How natural this seems to be
Is it really because of me?
Could it be you needing a diversion?
Or perhaps it's my unconscious perversion.
So who was it that encouraged who?
And what are we supposed to do?
           SINGLE ME AND MARRIED YOU
There must be a meaning or purpose to this
As we both sensed with our first touch and kiss
Attracted an attached to each other so fast
We must share something from the future or from the past
I didn't ask for you or you for me
But mystically **WE** caused **US** to be
           MARRIED YOU WITH SINGLE ME
Not sharing another today or tomorrow
Will definitely save us both future sorrow
Delusion, illusion and confusion are probabilities
Fate, destiny and bad timing are the realities
You and I seem such a Karmic match
Too bad we know there is that catch
SINGLE ME AND MARRIED YOU
           SO WHAT EXACTLY ARE WE TO DO?
           WE SHULDN'T BE YET HERE WE ARE
           GOING ON TO NOWHERE OR GOING VERY FAR

Guy – The End

Good Bye Guy!
Our drama is finally over and you ask why?
It's because the end ended with the beginning
Knowing no award we three would be winning
We lost integrity, lost time - I obviously lost my mind!

Bye, Bye Guy!
Both your wife and I are sick and tired of your lies
It's humiliating to continue to duck, dive and hide
We just missed her again having brunch on the east side
I confused my characters, got lost in the scene, no joy ride

'Good Bye' for *good* Guy!
It was a challenge, exciting and fun for a time, I won't deny
But the curtains came down, show is over – it's sad and I cry
Back to reality, no more lights, no more stars in my eyes
No more you, no more affairs, I need to keep what's left of my pride

Italian Nights

It's been many nights since we've been apart
Yet I still touch about for you in the dark
I used to use your shoulder to lay my head
I miss your warm body next to mine in bed
I miss hearing your heart beat
I miss our spoon and entwined feet
There's no one here now to dry my tears or calm my fears
I wake to hear myself scream out my pain, I call your name
My days now end with thoughts that are blue
As I face another night's sleep without you

Man on the Run

YOU'RE A MAN ON THE RUN
AFRAID OF HAVING TOO MUCH FUN
BECAUSE YOU KNOW I'M THE ONE

EACH TIME YOU SHOW THEN GO
WHAT YOU'RE DOING IS SO CLEAR
YOU'RE RUNNING FROM YOUR FEAR

WHY STILL CALL OR SEE ME AT ALL?
FORGET US! GO CHASE YOUR SUN
YOU'RE JUST A MAN ON THE RUN

You Let Me Fall

YOU DROPPED ME AT A TIME WHEN I NEEDED YOU MOST
IN MID-AIR I WAS LEFT DANGLING NAKED AND ALONE
SHIVERING FROM NO COMFORT OR WARMTH INSIDE OR OUT
I COULDN'T HOLD ON FOR TOO LONG
CRASHING HARD AGAINST LIFES REALITIES
YOU WERE NO LONGER THERE TO HELP ME DOWN OR
    CUSHION MY FALL
BROKEN, BRUISED AND BATTERED, I CRAWLED, THEN
    WALKED, THEN RAN
SAD, HURT AND ANGRY AT FINDING MYSELF IN SUCH A
    PAINFUL POSITION
HOW DID I GET DOWN THERE? YOU ONCE HAD ME WALKING
    UP ON AIR
NOW I REALLY CAN'T REMEMBER - AND I REALLY DON'T CARE
I NOT ONLY SURVIVED, I THRIVED WITHOUT YOU THERE
IT WASN'T EASY HEALING AND HAULING IT ALL ALONE
BUT I'M STRONG AND CAN FACE WHAT'S AROUND THE BEND
KNOWING I'LL NEVER GIVE MY FREEDOM UP TO GET SET UP
BY ANY MAN EVER, EVER AGAIN.

OTHERS

It's a Brick Wall Charlie

Slow down Charlie, you just hit a brick wall
Everyone heard and saw your downfall
Usually big men hide when they feel small
Instead you took a certain pride in it all

You choose to fight, always ready to clash
I watched you bleed from the huge gash
You said it wasn't there and I was talking trash
Can't accept that you alone caused your crash

You Deny, Deflect, Defy, and Dismiss
Hoping hurt goes away with a drink and a kiss

You now stumble when you once strode
Still trying to walk the rocky alcohol road
Lying and cheating is now your main mode
Your lined fine face belays your heavy load

You take everything too far, too fast
A grown bratty boy so loud and brash
Causing everyone to look at your bloody gash
Don't you realize you've finally run out of gas?

Yet, you Deny, Deflect, Defy and Dismiss
Wishing away your pain with a drink and a kiss

Bankers

Big chested
Barrel bellied
Big bucked Money Men
The U.S.is so full of them
who think thousand dollar threads and a
toni address entitle them to automatic access
any place, anytime, anything, just guess

White Face
Pink Hands
Fake tans and Asians
Bringing home big green
Trading amounts so obscene over the screen
with other greedy men who look like them all
have Devils eyes fixed on the prize - dollar signs

Maids clean
Nanny's care
Enormous egos have illicit affairs and
Buy wifey pricey things so she won't sing.
High living, stuffed shirts in stiff suits
Do what they do just because they can
So full of themselves those Banking men
And all U.S. Cities are so full of them.

Arthur Itis

MR. ARTHUR, LAST NAME ITIS CAME KNOCKING
SO SOFTLY I HARDLY KNEW HE WAS THERE
IT'S JUST ANOTHER GROWING ANNOYANCE
LIKE MY RAPIDLY GREYING BLACK HAIR

HE WAS TALKED OF IN THAT PERSONAL SWAY
OLD FOLKS SPOKE HIS NAME IN FAMILIAR TONES
THEY SAID ONE DAY HE'D COME MY WAY
AND GET DEEP DOWN INSIDE MY BONES

THEY SAID HE ALWAYS SHOWS WHEN IT RAINS
AND EVEN REMINDS YOU A DAY OR TWO BEFORE
BY SENDING YOU STIFFNESS, ACHES AND PAINS
WHILE KNOCKING LOUDLY AT YOUR DOOR

NOW FOR SURE I DON'T WANT HIM VISITING
ARTHUR'S NO ONE I'D WANT TO BE MY FRIEND
HE'S ALREADY STOLEN MY EASE OF MOTION
AND HE'S UPSETTING MY ENERGY AND EMOTIONS

CONTROLLING, INFLICTING PAIN IS HIS ONLY WAY
ATTACKING JOINTS IS NOT THE WAY TO PLAY
I DIDN'T KNOW ONCE HE CAME HE'D COME TO STAY
ARTHUR ITIS MUST BE STOPPED AND LOCKED AWAY

Rush To Oz Rodney

Mr. Lion, now how are you going to get to OZ acting all weepy like this?
My friend, you need to run and see the Wizard cause you done lost it!
You're up here hiding behind trees, crying in the woods, that's not
   doing you no good.
For too many years you've been fronting but not doing what you
   should.
It's time to pull yourself together and get on your way. Please, do not
   delay!
From where you are now, getting your courage certificate is far, far
   away

Now don't try to follow that cute but clueless, country Dorothy
She only cares about her shiny red shoes and Toto any darn way
Don't spend a minuet with the simple Straw Man who can't even think
And don't revive the rusty, weird Tin Man - just let him squeak and
   clink
The scary cat you are, you'll want to get to OZ before darkness comes
   down
Walking there at night, you'll hear tigers, bears and lots of unknown
   sounds

Go On! You have no time to wait for friends to walk you through the
   forest
They will slow you down with their own issues - you cannot even stop
   for a rest!
Quit stalling for time, you need to get to OZ and see the wizard quick
You're a Lion, a beast, king of the forest and need to start acting like it!

Don't stop to smell flowers in the field that makes you high and slow

Pretty witch Glenda's not floating in to help you just so you know

The green faced bitch on the broom is zooming around looking to snatch you up too

If you try to help Dorothy find her busy little dog, something bad can happen to You!

Flying monkeys will nip at your tail and pull tuffs from your mangy mane

Hurry on and run as fast as you can down that long, yellow brick lane

Head straight to the castle on the hill, cross the moat - you can make it if you try

Bang hard on the big doors to get in and don't let that sham of a man make you cry

Ask the 'All Powerful Wizard' to give you a badge of courage and a *makeover* too!

Then walk proudly back as **'King of the Forest'** knowing that title now suits you

Run, Run, Run

Run, Run, Run
Fish are gonna swim, birds must fly
You gotta run and don't even know why

Running, Running, Running
Like you're being chased, hunted with a gun
A long time ago, the running game was fun
Playtime is over; all your playmates went home
You're still out running while all your friends got grown
They're busy with their lives; you have nothing of your own

Still you Run, Run, Run
Day and night you run from right in all cases
Into deep dark places where no one's wearing faces

Fear keeps you Running, Running, Running
Like life was an endless Marathon
Afraid to look behind you, just gotta keep moving on
It's been so very long now, you forgot or never knew
The only one you're running against, from or to is YOU!!!

Mr. Man

HE'S BEEN A MAN FOR A VERY LONG TIME
WHAT A SHAME, WHAT A CRIME
I WAS HOPING HE'D BE A BIT OF A BOY
WITH TRAITS OF INNOCENCE AND JOY
WHILE STILL BEING THE MAN THAT HE MUST BE
HE'S SO REAL TO HIM AND SO FAKE TO ME
MISTER MAN, MISTER MAN WHY DOES HE LIVE HIS LIFE AS A
    SHAM?

They are Veterans

THEY ARE YOUNG, THEY DECIDE
THEY ENLIST, THEY HAVE PRIDE
THEY TRAIN HARD, THEY GET TOUGH
THEY ACCEPT, THEY LIVE ROUGH
THEY ARE STRONG FOR US

THEY HAVE FEAR, THEY HAVE FIGHT
THEY STRIVE ON, THEY BOND TIGHT
THEY PROTECT AND THEY DEFEND
THEY SIGN UP AGAIN AND AGAIN
THEY ARE BRAVE FOR US

THEY WRITE HOME, THEY CRY
THEY HAVE KIDS, THEY PROVIDE
THEY LAUGH, THEY PLAY
THEY HURT, THEY PRAY
THEY HAVE LOVE FOR US

THEY KILL, THEY SEE HORROR
THEY FEEL GUILT, THEY KNOW HONOR
THEY COME HOME, THEY ARE MAIMED
THEY SUCCEED, THEY GO INSANE

THEY DON'T COME HOME, THEY ARE MISSING
THEY ARE DEAD, BURIED HEAD TO HEAD
THEY ARE FATHERS, MOTHERS, HUSBANDS, WIVES
THEY ARE THANKED FOR GIVING US THEIR LIVES
THEY ARE ALWAYS REMEMBERD NOT JUST TODAY
THE DEEP RESPECT I HAVE WILL NEVER GO AWAY
THEY ARE MISSED, THEY ARE LOVED, THEY ARE VETERANS

Their World

The Hippies

It's like a big bright beautiful red top
But it's slightly chipped on one side
The children don't like it
They want it to spin on its side
It's not doing it yet
So the children kick at this top
(You'd never know it's been spinning that way all along)
But these children are different
These children are unique
They have new and changing ideas
The top is staying the same
It's not spinning on its side
It's not spinning upside down yet.
So the children continue to abuse this beautiful chipped top
Which is the WORLD.

LOSS & PAIN

Why?

Why do sweet grapes turn sour?
Why do flowers droop then die?
Why did our love turn to hate?
Why do things change? Why?

What did I do to lose love with you?
I tried to coincide with your mind
Did not hold on to you too tight
So you could move and feel right
I learned to accept not to expect a thing from you
And not a thing or respect was what I got is true

I trusted your emphatic words
I believed the sincere promises
I confused your lust with love
You showered me with affection
Your actions hid your intentions
Until there was a change in your direction

Just as juicy grapes turn sour
And how dry a once fresh flower
Time ran out on our happy hour
Why did this have to happen?

Why can't we stop the rain?
Why can't we cure our pain?
Why do things in life have to change?
Why?

Still Grieving

About My Dad

AS I LAY ON MY BACK ON THE COLD EARTH DIRT
GASPING FOR FRESH AIR, ANY AIR. I CAN'T
CRY, SCREAM OR BREATHE
I FEEL I'M ALL BOXED IN BY A GLASS COFFIN NO ONE ELSE SEES
EYES GLAZED OVER WIDE, WATCHING
WITHOUT KNOWING WHY
HANDS CLAWING AT WHAT I CAN'T SEE, PUSHING AGAINST
WHAT I CAN'T SEEM TO MOVE OUT OF MY WAY
I HAVE NO STRENGTH - I HAVE NO WILL
EVERY ONCE IN A BLUE MOON, I CATCH A GLIMPSE
OF DARK SKY OR BLACK STAR PASSING BY
SOMETHING I CAN'T UNDERSTAND, TUGS HARDER
AND GETS HEAVIER ON MY HEART EVERY DAY
SOMETHING I DON'T KNOW THROWS CLOUDS
IN MY EYES SO I CAN'T SEE CLEARLY NOW
SOMETHING I CAN'T HEAR FILLS MY HEAD WITH
SOUNDS SO I CAN'T THINK ANYMORE
I'M SO TIRED OF FIGHTING MY WAY
THROUGH THIS INVISIBLE WAR
JUST TRYING TO SURVIVE, NOTHING MORE
BUT I CAN'T MOVE – I HAVE NO WILL
I DO LONG TO BE AWARE AND ALIVE
ALONG WITH EVERYONE ELSE
BUT NOW I'M FLAT ON MY BACK LIKE
A BABY NEEDING A CHANGE
MY ONLY GOAL IS TO STAND AGAIN. TO
WALK, TALK AND SMILE, NOT CRY
YET I CAN'T SEEM TO ACCEPT, I CAN'T
SEEM TO FORGET ALTHOUGH I TRY
I'M STILL CONSUMED AND ENTOMED
WITH HEAVY INTENSE GRIEF
AND MY NAILS STILL BLEED FROM EFFORTS MADE
TO GET OUT, NOT QUITE COMPLETE.

Ump, Ump, Ump

That was the year we would like to have skipped
A dysfunctional family but close and tight knit

The beginning was cold and cruel to our clan
It all but put down our strongest go-to man
Who survived the mean streets and Viet Nam
Ump, Ump, Ump, it's a stinkin shame
A disease has put him in a chair with wheels
Why Him? Why this? Why mobility to steal?
Ump, Ump, Ump seemed to answer it all

The summer gave reason to be hopeful and glad
My Ivy League bound nephew was a high school grad
A collected sigh of relief, a solid future to be had
Ump, Ump, Ump, it's a stinkin shame we said with a smile
So many talents, so many skills he has yet to explore
Which one? Which way? A world with open doors
Ump, Ump, Ump just said it all

In the fall, family was shocked and forced to bare
Life slipped quickly away from our beloved so dear
Red caddy, classy, wore one gold curl in her hair
Ump, Ump, Ump, what a stinkin shame we all cried
How could this be? How will we go on? She was our pride
So sunny, so funny, quirky, talented and unique
Ms. Church Lady, successful, the family history she'd keep
Ump, Ump, Ump, from the depths of our throats
Ump, Ump, Ump was all we *could* say

Less laughter to have, to hear – all in one year
Empty seats, fewer hands to hold in prayer
Family traditions now changed, re-arranged
Even Michael Jackson overnight disappeared
Ump, Ump, Ump, it was a stinkin shame
Ump, Ump, Ump we said with such pain
That *was* the year – Ump, Ump, Ump

Why are so Many Going There?

Wait. What? I can't believe what I just read
Seems no matter which way I turn my head
Someone is gone, killed, someone is dead

Every time I seem to turn around
Someone is lowered into the ground
Someone's ashes are spread around
Another someone's loved one down

It's one right after another, I'd like to catch my breath
There's been too many senseless untimely deaths
People were just here then quietly got up and left
Leaving all of us stunned, sad, extremely bereft

They walked through the door that said, 'RETURN NO MORE'
So many rushing to it like a super sale at a store
It seems not to matter which way I turn my head
Somebody's loved one is gone, someone is dead

It's not just old age or those with a terminal disease
Its accidents, hate and drive by's. Strong drugs, weak hearts and legal
genocide. Its immature minds, illegal guns and those choosing suicide.
And sadly, far too many are far too young to have died

Yes, every time I turn my head and look around
A casket is buried into the ground
Loved one's ashes shared and spread around
Family, friends, famous fleeing life, falling down

I'd like to catch my breath from knowing of so much death

Waiting in Vain

I WISH YOU'D COME AND GET ME
I'M SITTING HERE WAITING FOR YOU
I HAVE FOOD TO EAT AND WINE TO DRINK
AND SEVERAL THINGS TO DO

SURE WISH YOU'D COME AND TAKE ME
PERHAPS MAYBE YOU HAVE FORGOT
I'VE BEEN SITTING HERE SO LONG ALONE
STILL HERE IN THE VERY SAME SPOT

YOU TOLD ME YOU'D NEVER LEAVE ME
SO I'M NOT WORRIED YET
YOU TOLD ME YOU REALLY LOVED ME
SO I KNOW YOU COULD NOT FORGET.

STILL WISH YOU'D COME AND GET ME
BECAUSE THE NIGHTS ARE GETTING CHILLY
THE FOOD WENT BAD, THE WINES BEEN HAD
AND NOW I'M BORED AND SILLY

IF ONLY YOU'D COME AND TAKE ME
EVERY THING WILL BE OKAY
WE CAN STILL MAKE LOVE TOGETHER
BEFORE WE BOTH TURN OLD AND GREY

Time to Move On

Time To Can The Laughter
Time To Bottle The Tears
Time To Pack The Memories
That Get Heavy Through The Years
File The Fun and Sunshine For a Sad and Gloomy Day
And All The Pain and Heartache Can Just Be Thrown Away
It's So Hard To Let Go of Things You've Always Known
But Looking At Your Past Shows How Much You've Grown

Women of Courage

Woman of the Wilderness

It seems, Native woman walks alone
The cold, stark wilderness is home
Perfectly safe, warm and protected is she
The idea of fear is an unknown quality
Living with all of earths creatures and non-resistant
She is constantly in a state of peaceful acceptance
A storm is no bother since it is only an expected other

Always prepared on the frontier, because one knows
How bitter and hard winter winds always blow
Earth bound woman wrapped deep in hide of buffalo
Thick fur around her neck already adorned with leather strings
Strung of teeth and bones for strength and courage
Her hat is the hollowed head of the brave black bear
It covers feathers from eagles wings braided into her hair
Steady feet are swathed in warm lamb skin and soft squirrel fur

Together, the moon and a million stars light her way in the dark
Wise white snow owls act as alarms throughout the thick woods
Although no beast goes near with any intention to harm her
Being one with nature, there is a natural respect of space out here
Knowing her land, she borrows from the earth to make medicines
That will heal someone in need on the other side of the wilderness
Native woman never walks alone. Shadows are always before, beside
    and behind her
The shadows are her air bound ancestors, still walking silently along
    their paths

Grandma Emma Elizabeth Medley Hatcher

Aunt Rosalie Hatcher Hall Holmes

A Warm Iron at Her Feet

To My Aunt Rosalie

You told me as a young girl a long time ago
You stared death in the face but you did not know
Your Dear Momma was about to go
She just had my Dad, your baby Brother only six months ago

She said she was cold, smiled and sighed
Your Brother Bill knew and ran outside
You went and warmed an iron to place at her feet
At just sixteen, the gesture was so loving, so sweet
Trying to bring back your Mother with a warm iron at her feet

Looking back on your long and well lived life
You were such a lady, loving family member and wife
I admired your accomplishments, sense of adventure and style
Always gracious, religious, you loved to laugh and smile
Your natural harmony and beauty came through in everything you'd do
I learned to be proud, strong and independent because of you

But when I last saw you My Aunt just the other day
Your gaze was already far, far away
Holding so many words you could no longer say
I was staring death in the eye, not knowing how to say goodbye
We squeezed each others hand and I cried

So as I see you now in your peaceful eternal sleep
I think of placing a warm iron at your feet
Wishing to bring back my Aunt with a warm iron at her feet.

The Little Girl in Pink

One day sitting in my car outside class, I had an assignment to complete
and fast
A quick glance in my rearview mirror showed a small figure walking
slowly in the street
Sandwiched between the parked and fast passing cars from behind her
Oblivious to any possible danger, as if in a trance, she dragged her feet
while walking in the street

Little girl dressed in pink
What is it that you think?

So curious, I watched and noticed neat braids ending in bright pink
beads under a pink hat
She wore a pink puffy, pink sneakers and had a pink Dora backpack
From across the street, I viewed a child staring straight ahead
An expressionless face like one of the living dead

The little girl in pink
Sure made me think

Pink printed gloves hung from her coat sleeves on that cold day
I squinted then gasped as I saw what she'd been doing the whole way
Her bare little hand ran along each car end to end
Has she done this before? Will she do this again?
She seemed to deliberately, delicately caress each one
Does she have any friends? Is there trouble at home?

This girl pretty in pink
Is very special I think

Watching that strange child's strange walk in the street
Made me late to class and my assignment *Incomplete*!

Winged Victory Woman

I AM AN ALUMNI OF GHS

Sometimes I feel like a Soldier in battle
Barely dodging mind fields underfoot
At times I'm a Fireman fighting flames
Erupting all around, surrounding me
And I can feel like a Policeman trying
to maintain order out of chaos in my life
I feel I'm a Doctor diagnosing myself
And always attempting to treat someone else
Then I'm a Teacher, a Preacher sharing the
good I know because I'm daring to care
But it's the times when I feel small, or feel like I've failed
When I'm in need of a hug, a hand, an assurance of Yes You Can
That I remember, I'm also Winged Victory standing proudly alone
Bare feet firmly planted on solid ground
I remember I have power, and wings to fly over, under or around any
    obstacle ever found
Remember, Winged Victory is a Headless Woman who cannot feel
the weight of the many hats I wear
Nor can she ever see, hear, speak, do evil or feel the loads I bare
I'm a Girls High Girl and like Winged Victory, a Fearless Warrior
I am Strong, Intelligent and Beautiful while being Faceless
So I am Ageless, Raceless, and most times Fameless
I am and you too are a Winged Victory Woman, Victorious now and
    Always. Remember?

At Last

Hallelujah time
Alone under the painted tree
Shout, laugh, cry freedom

Sharing its color
Sun sets reluctantly slow
Healing waters flow

Made it over hills
Through deep valleys to be here
Grateful to see God

Sky high cotton clouds
Magic multi-colored leaves
Fragrant flowers bloom

Forgetting time past
New beginnings ahead now
Victory is mine

Appendix

Arthur Itis - Mount Vernon, NY 05.18.2014

Atlantic City at Night, The Chair - Atlantic City, NJ 03.06.1995

Atlantic City at Night, The Waves – Atlantic City, NJ 08.01.1991

At Last – Mount Vernon, NY 09.30.2014
Photo: "From The Mountain Top", oil & collage on paper by Benny Andrews

A Message To You – Mount Vernon, NY 09.24.2014

A Poem For Right Now, Covid 19 – Mount Vernon, NY 03.20.2020

A Sudden Storm – Mount Vernon, NY 02-2012

A Warm Iron at Her Feet, In Honor of my Aunt Rosalie Hatcher Hall
     Philadelphia, PA 09.15-25.1991
Photo: Family Archive, Grandma Emma Elizabeth Medley Hatcher

Bankers – New York, NY 03.2011

Beauty in a Hard Place – Mount Vernon, NY 10.11.2016
Photo: Dona Elena Hatcher @ Third St, Mount Vernon, NY 2016

Beer for Breakfast – Mount Vernon, NY 09.30.2013

Before My Very Eyes – New York, NY 04.04.1982

Deep Sea Love – Millersville, PA 11.14.1975
Picture: Dona Elena Hatcher, Hand colored with pencils 2018

Fallen Feather – Mount Vernon, NY 08.27.2012

Guy, the Beginning – New York, NY 04.28.1992

Guy, the Middle – New York, NY 04.28.1992

Guy, the End – New York, NY 04.28.1992

If Only For A Day – Philadelphia, PA 04.07.2001
Photo: Family Archive of Daddy & Me, 1956

Italian Nights – Milan, Italy 1985

It's a Brick Wall Charlie – Mount Vernon, NY 07.16.2011

Little Girl in Pink – Mount Vernon, NY 05.26.2016

Morning – Mount Vernon, NY 06.02.2013

Mr. Man – Los Angeles, CA 01.10.1993

My Moment With A Mole – Mount Vernon, NY 04.14.2019

My Backyard Grass – Mount Vernon, NY 10.02.2013

One Blade of Grass – Philadelphia, PA 1970

River Running or Mitch from LA – Philadelphia, PA 2000

Run, Run, Run — New York, NY 09.05.2008
Rush To Oz Rodney — New York, NY 05.28.2008
Shadow Man — New York, NY 02.08.1983
Photo: Unknown from Facebook
Still Grieving — Philadelphia, PA 06.04.1997
Stone Man — New York, NY 03.05.2000
Stray Dogs — New York, NY 03.26.2009
Summertime — Mount Vernon, NY 06.2011
The Heights, Thought #1 — New York, NY 10.25.2007
The Heights Thought #2 — New York, NY 03.2011
They Are Veterans — Mount Vernon, NY 11.2011
Time To Move On — Millersville, PA 08.12.1975
Ump, Ump, Ump! — Mount Vernon, NY 09.15.2014
Waves — Atlantic City, NJ 09.27.1968
Why? — Millersville, PA mid 1970's
Why is Everybody Going There? — Mount Vernon, NY 04.25.2016
Whoosh! — New York, NY 02.2011
Woman of the Wilderness — Mount Vernon, NY 10.15.2014 (inspired by the
    art of Shaman Calendar, "Bear Woman" 1986)
You Let Me Fall — New York, NY mid 1990's

Cover Design and Book Layout: Josep Book Designs
Back Photo: Selfie by Dona Elena Hatcher, Rye, NY 09.25.2020

Biography

Dona Elena Hatcher is a Libra Drama Queen born and raised in Philadelphia, PA. Her Mother's musical family had deep roots in Mount Vernon, NY dating back to the early 1900's. Her Father's family were long time property owners from South Egg Harbor, NJ. As a child, Dona and her sister split the summers between both families plus a 2 week annual rental on Wildwood Beach, NJ.

Dona began writing at 5 years old and produced neighborhood musicals at 13. She credits early travel, music, art, ballet classes and National Geographic magazines for stimulating her lifelong work in creative arts. She attended the famous Philadelphia High School for Girls then Millersville State University.

She moved to NYC in 1980, then to Los Angeles in 1994 to study and further her acting and modeling career. Dona worked a variety of exciting freelance jobs while doing so. Throughout her many foreign and domestic travel experiences, she wrote poems expressing her thoughts. Dona has been published in several anthologies, newspapers and magazines. She belonged to many Performance Poetry Groups on both coasts.

Dona now owns and lives in the cottage that belonged to her Grandmother in Mount Vernon, New York, a close NYC suburb and is a 5 star Airbnb Hostess.

A professional Actress, Model, Makeup Artist and Crafter, Dona is a long time member of the Screen Actors Guild and American

Federation of Radio and Television Artist. She has 100's of film, TV, radio and magazine credits.

From 2017 through 2019, Dona feels blessed to have survived an Aortic Aneurysm, a Heart Valve replacement, Bypass surgery, Brevi Virus Infection and AFIB. Miraculously, she quickly bounced back and everything is now in right rhythm.

Currently, Dona owns *Take Flight Talent Workshops* where she instructs beginning Actors and Models of all ages. She also is the Creator of *Second Chance Cans*, uniquely hand decorated recycled household cans.

"WORD DANCES - POEMS ON POINTE!" is her first solo Poetry Picture Book.